Funny Faces TO DRAW

Illustrated by Neal Yamamoto
Text by Amy Margaret

LOWELL HOUSE JUVENILE
LOS ANGELES
NTC/Contemporary Publishing Group

NOTE: The numbered eraser in the upper right-hand corner of each project indicates the level of difficulty—1 being the easiest and 3 the hardest.

Published by Lowell House
A division of NTC/Contemporary Publishing Group, Inc.
4255 West Touhy Avenue, Lincolnwood (Chicago), Illinois 60712 U.S.A.

Copyright © 2000 by NTC/Contemporary Publishing Group, Inc.
All rights reserved. No part of this work may be reproduced, stored in a retrieval system, or transmitted in any form or by any means, electronic, mechanical, photocopying, recording, or otherwise, without the prior permission of NTC/Contemporary Publishing Group, Inc. Requests for such permissions should be sent to the address above.

Managing Director and Publisher: Jack Artenstein
Director of Publishing Services: Rena Copperman
Editorial Director: Brenda Pope-Ostrow
Director of Art Production: Bret Perry
Designer: Victor Perry

Library of Congress Catalog Card Number: 00-130073
ISBN 0-7373-0479-0

Lowell House books can be purchased at special discounts when ordered in bulk for premiums and special sales. Contact Customer Service at the address above, or call 1-800-323-4900.

Printed and bound in the United States of America
VH 10 9 8 7 6 5 4 3 2 1

Contents

1. Baby Boo 4
2. Count Korba 6
3. Mean Jean Daluca 8
4. Wallace the Waiter 9
5. Romeo DeGiorgio 10
6. Eggie Joe .12
7. Howling Harry 14
8. Ben Willard 15
9. Louie the Lion 16
10. Princess Kewpie 18
11. Joey the Eye 20
12. Grannie Mae 21
13. Battlin' Maxie 22
14. G.I. Gene .24
15. Igor Jr. 26
16. Monstress Maude 27
17. Pirate Pete 28
18. Val Kyrie .30
19. Grin Kong 32
20. Toucan Bill 34
21. Bud O'Hare 35
22. Merlo the Mentalist 36
23. Hard Hat Hank 38
24. Sous Chef Sue 40
25. Wild-Eyed Wally 42
26. Nikki Nak 43
27. Angry Angus 44
28. Goof the Clown 46
29. King Lou .48
30. Pat T. O'Brien 50
31. Thrasher Dude 52
32. I. B. Yeller 53
33. Suzie Q. 54
34. The Doctor's Monster 56
35. Ye Olde Pilgrim 58
36. Proboscis Pete 60
37. Ralphus Cattus 62
38. Gustavus Goof 63
39. Ol' Doc Lang 64
40. Ho-Hum Henry 65
41. Mrs. Doldrums 66
42. Johnny Angel 68
43. Icthyus Imp 70
44. Skull Twister 71
45. 'Lectric Man 72
46. Screamin' Mimi 74
47. Whistlin' Willy 75
48. Hysterical Hap 76
49. Frannie Fan 78
50. Hairy Dan 80

Baby Boo

BABY BOO IS CUCKOO!
(BUT IT'S NOT HIS FAULT—HE WAS BORN THAT WAY.)

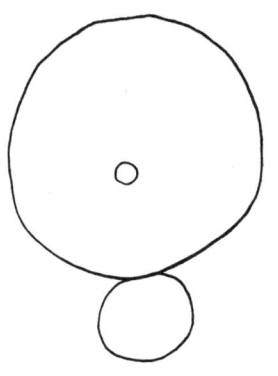

1. Draw a large circle for Baby Boo's head and a small one inside it for the nose. Draw a little circle beneath the head for the body.

2. Above the nose, draw two connecting round shapes for the baby's crazy eyes. Draw a horizontal line extending beyond the circle as shown.

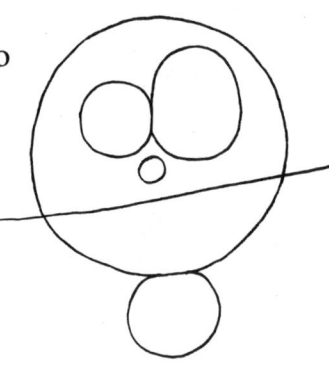

3. Add two dots in the eyes for pupils. Sketch two oval-shaped ears on either side of Baby Boo's head.

4. Draw two big teeth coming from the baby's mouth. Begin to detail the ears.

5. Sketch in feet and arms. Add a smaller rounded shape next to the big tooth. This will be the open mouth. Add eyebrows.

6. Begin to draw toes on the feet, as well as finger and thumb shapes on the ends of the arms. Add a curlicue hairdo and the corners of the mouth.

7. Add a diaper and two more toes on each foot.

8. Erase unneeded lines in the feet. Fill in the mouth. Don't forget to add the belly button!

Count Korba

COUNT KORBA MAY LOOK BORED, BUT HE'S ACTUALLY A SPY WITH MORE MYSTERIOUS SECRETS THAN YOU COULD IMAGINE!

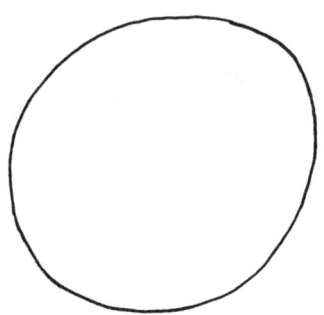

1. Draw a large circle. This will become the lower portion of his face.

2. Add a smaller half-circle on top of the large one. Draw a little circle in the large circle for the count's nose. Suggest shoulders with short lines on either side of the large circle. Begin a jacket with two slightly curved lines under his chin.

3. Begin to detail his face. Draw slits for eyes, and two partial ovals on either side of his nose and his forehead. Add a little downturned mouth.

4. Continue detailing his eyes and ears.

5. Add hair, a mustache, and eyebrows. Draw little pupils under his eyelids.

6. Add stripes on his shirt and an eyepiece around one of his eyes.

7. Erase unneeded lines, and fill in his pupils and jacket. Add a thin chain running down from his eyepiece.

7

 # Mean Jean Daluca

YOU'D FEEL MEAN, TOO, IF YOUR MOTHER MADE YOU WEAR A BIG PONYTAIL ON TOP OF YOUR HEAD ALL THE TIME!

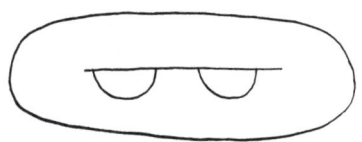

1. Draw a wide oval shape. Then sketch a horizontal line in the center of it with two half-circles coming from it. These are Mean Jean's eyes.

2. Add pupils and eyebrows. Then sketch her nose and small downturned mouth.

3. Begin to outline her hair, and add a neck.

4. Detail her face with freckles. Finish outlining her hair, and don't forget to add that "perky" ponytail on top.

5. Fill in her hair and pupils. Add a cute collar around Mean Jean's neck. (She hates that, too!)

 # Wallace the Waiter

THIS FUN FACE IS A GREAT DOODLE TO DRAW ON ANY PAPER PLACE MAT.

1. First draw a pencil shape, rounded at the top and pointed on the bottom. Begin to draw the face with two eyes and a nose.

2. Add his ears and mouth. Sketch his hair part. Suggest the waiter's shoulders as shown.

3. Outline the rest of his hair, and add a pointed collar around his neck.

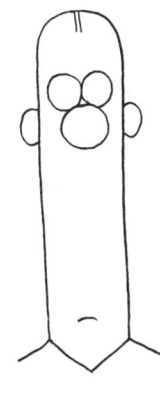

4. Give Wallace pupils and a pencil-thin mustache. Begin to draw his bow tie on top of his collar.

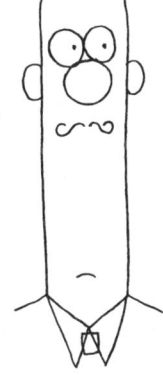

5. Detail his ears, and give him eyebrows. Finish the bow tie.

6. Fill in his hair, and shade his bow tie. Erase any lines you don't need in his collar and bow tie.

 # Romeo DeGiorgio

WHEN GEORGIE PORGIE KISSED THE GIRLS, HE MADE THEM CRY.
WITH HIS LARGE SCHNOZ, ROMEO JUST POKES THEM IN THE EYE!

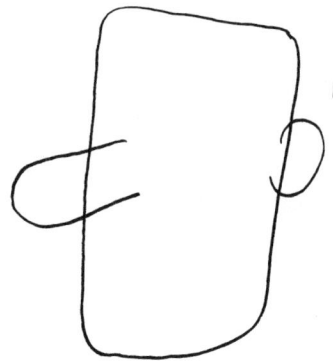

1. Draw a rectangular shape with rounded edges. Add an ear and a long nose.

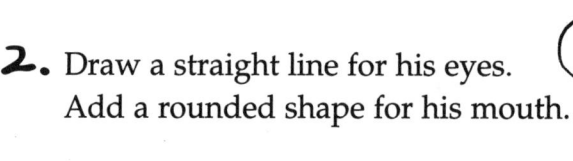

2. Draw a straight line for his eyes. Add a rounded shape for his mouth.

3. Add eyes, and suggest a forehead. Sketch a nostril and puckered lips. Draw a neck.

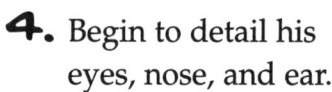

4. Begin to detail his eyes, nose, and ear.

5. Start to outline his hair. Add eyebrows and a small crease between his eyes.

6. Continue to outline all his hair, including his funky sideburns.

7. Complete sketching his hair with a flip at his neck.

8. Fill in his hair and pupils, and erase all unneeded lines.

Eggie Joe

JOE GOT THIS WAY FROM EATING TOO MANY EGGS, EGGPLANT, AND EGG-CELENT CHOCOLATE CAKE!

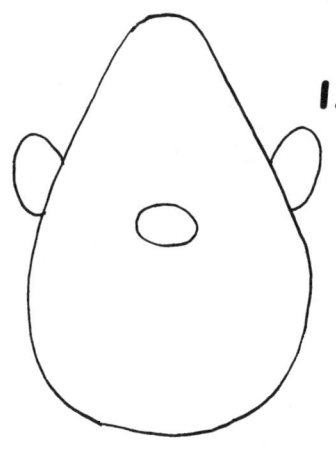

1. Begin with a pear shape for his head. Add two ears and a nose.

2. Add his eyes and a nose ring.

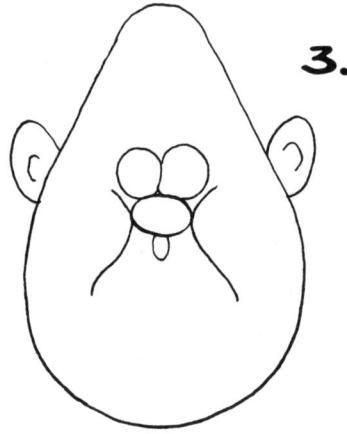

3. Indicate his chubby cheeks as shown, and begin to detail his ears.

4. Draw crescent shapes around his eyes. Sketch a slightly curved mouth.

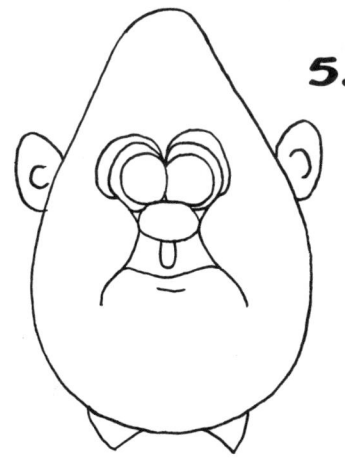

5. Add another set of crescents around his eyes and a small line under his mouth. Indicate a collar.

6. Draw thick eyebrows and wrinkles on his forehead. Dot in two tiny pupils. Begin to draw a necktie at his collar. Indicate a chin.

7. Finish his necktie, and add a small tuft of hair on his head.

8. Fill in his tie and hair.

Howling Harry

WHEN HOWLING HARRY SEES A LONG-LOST BUD, HE LOVES TO HOWL, "HELLOOOO!"

1. Draw a long rectangle with slightly rounded corners. Sketch two circles for his eyes.

2. Add ears and a wide, howling mouth.

3. Detail eyes, ears, and mouth.

4. Suggest cheeks and a small nose. Finish detailing ears. Add hair across his forehead and a tongue in his mouth.

5. Fill in the back of Harry's mouth and his hair.

Ben Willard

BEN CAN HEAR HARRY'S HOWLING "HELLOOOO" FROM ANYWHERE!

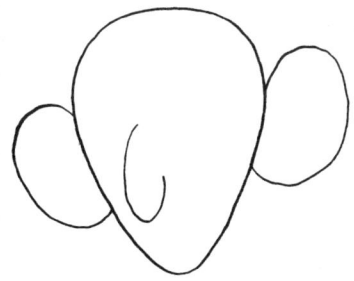

1. Draw an upside-down teardrop shape. Add a hooked nose and two huge ears.

2. Add two small eyes, a mouth, and curved lines in the ears.

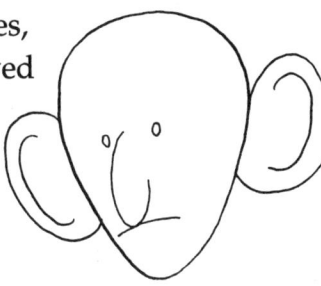

3. Add another set of curved lines in the ears. Draw eyebrows and large teeth. Begin to detail the eyes.

4. Indicate a full head of hair, and add a neck.

5. Fill in the hair, eyebrows, and eyes, shading the eyes slightly.

 # Louie the Lion

ON YOUR OWN, YOU CAN GIVE LOUIE—THE "MANE" MAN—A CRAZY ANIMAL BODY.

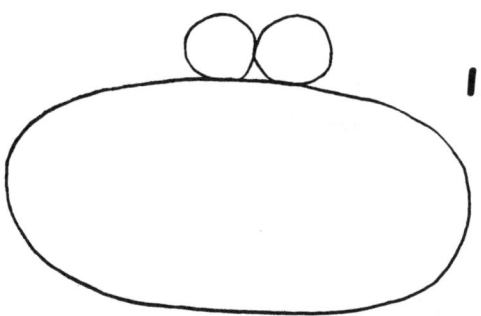

1. Draw a flat oval and two circles on top of it for the eyes.

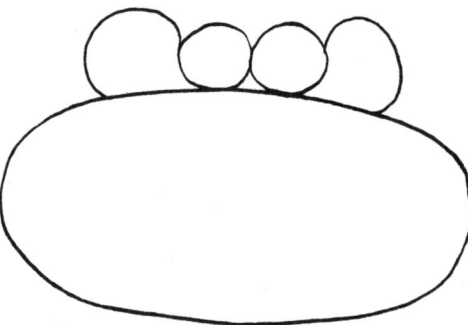

2. On either side of Louie's eyes, sketch ears.

3. Begin to detail the ears, and add pupils. Draw a triangle for the nose.

4. Connect the nose to the top of the oval with two lines.

5. Add the wide mouth and tongue.

6. Begin to draw the mane, and add a line in the tongue.

7. Give Louie whiskers, and finish outlining the mane.

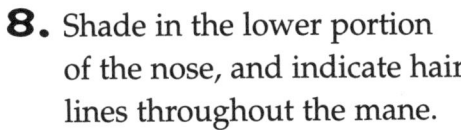

8. Shade in the lower portion of the nose, and indicate hair lines throughout the mane.

 # Princess Kewpie

PRINCESS KEWPIE WOULD BE A CUTE ADDITION TO ANY SWEET BIRTHDAY CARD.

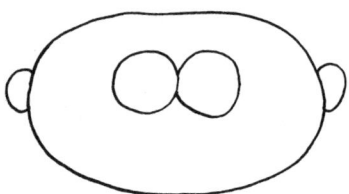

1. Draw a wide oval, and sketch Princess Kewpie's ears and eyes.

2. Add her little upturned nose. Suggest her royal robe.

3. Finish outlining her robe. Draw her mouth.

4. Detail her ears, including earrings. Add pupils and eyelashes to her eyes, and give the princess cutie-pie lips.

5. Begin to detail her robe and crown.

6. Continue detailing her robe and crown. Begin to sketch her hair.

7. Continue drawing her hair and crown.

8. Finish outlining her hair, and add jewels to the top of her crown.

9. Erase unneeded lines, and fill in her eyes and earrings. Finish her hair, and she is ready to rule!

Joey the Eye

ONCE YOU FINISH JOEY THE EYE, HOW ABOUT CREATING YOUR OWN LINE OF JOEY CHARACTERS? TRY JOEY THE NOSE, JOEY THE HAIR, AND EVEN JOEY THE FOOT!

1. Begin with an irregular shape for the head. Then draw Joey's famous eyes.

2. Add a small triangle for his nose and two ears.

3. Draw an oval for his open mouth, and add a hair curl on his forehead.

4. Begin to detail his eyes with brows, his mouth with a tongue, and his ears as shown. Indicate a chin.

5. Sketch a thin neck and more hair.

6. Erase the unneeded line in his chin. Fill in his hair, nose, and mouth.

Grannie Mae

LOVABLE, SQUISHABLE GRANNIE MAE IS EVERYONE'S FAVORITE GRANDMA TO DRAW.

1. Begin Grannie's large face with a slightly flattened circle. Then sketch a half-circle on top of it. Indicate her dress with small half-circles.

2. Add a nose and the one ear that is showing.

3. Begin to draw her hair and spectacles.

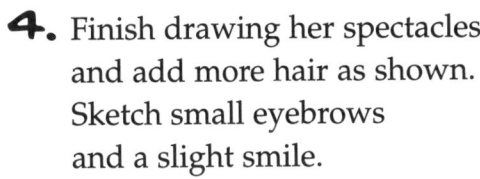

4. Finish drawing her spectacles, and add more hair as shown. Sketch small eyebrows and a slight smile.

5. Add eyelashes around the spectacles, and indicate her chin. Draw more hair on her forehead.

6. Erase any unneeded lines, and fill in her hair.

 # Battlin' Maxie

THIS SILLY CHARACTER LOVES TO FIGHT . . . WITH HIMSELF! HE GIVES HIMSELF THE MEANEST RIGHT HOOK, LEAVING A BLACK EYE EVERY TIME.

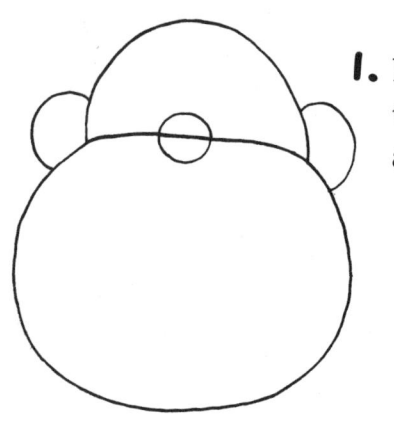

1. Draw a circle, slightly flattened on top. Add a half-circle on top of it. This will be Battlin' Maxie's face. Sketch two ears, and begin his nose.

2. Add his nostrils on either side of his nose. Begin to detail his ears.

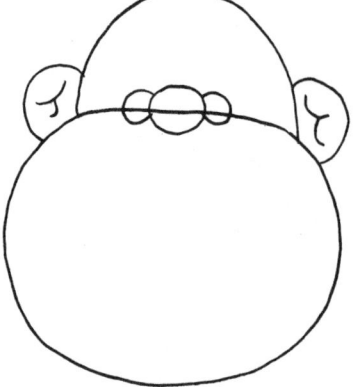

3. Draw his eyes, one half-open and the other completely closed. Start to draw his cheeks.

4. Below the cheek lines, draw a large openmouthed grin. Add a pupil in his eye and thick eyebrows above both eyes.

5. Add a bruise underneath his closed eye, and draw a thin line above the closed eye to show its swelling. Put teeth in his mouth.

6. Draw a small vertical line right under his nose, as well as a couple of scalloped lines to show wrinkles between his eyes. Draw a squarish jaw.

7. Indicate his chin with a small horizontal line under his mouth and a vertical one for a chin cleft. To show Maxie's bandanna, draw the two ends on either side of his head.

8. Finally, fill in his bruise, pupil, eyebrows, and one tooth. Erase the unnecessary lines, and further detail the bandanna. Watch out as Battlin' Maxie goes for another punch!

G.I. Gene

G.I. GENE IS A LEAN, MEAN, EXTREME MACHINE—BY THE WAY, HE'S ALSO GREEN!

1. Begin Gene with a square shape, wider and slightly rounded on the bottom. Draw a long, thin rim for his helmet.

2. Add the helmet on top of his head, and show his neck with a wide, short triangle.

3. Draw his eyes and ears.

4. Add pupils to his eyes, and detail his ears. Draw his long nose and nostrils.

5. Sketch small circles inside his pupils, and add a mustache. Draw a stripe going around his helmet.

6. Add an upside-down *V* above the stripe on his helmet. Begin to show hair between the helmet and his ears. Indicate a growling mouth below the mustache.

7. Draw diagonal stripes running behind the designs on the helmet. Add a little more hair below the ears. Give his mouth more growl with teeth and a facial line.

8. Continue to detail his helmet with more lines going in the opposite direction. Sketch hairs in his mustache, and give G.I. Gene a collar.

9. Erase any lines you don't need, and fill in his pupils, leaving the small circles white. Color his hair however you wish—especially green!

Igor Jr.

EVERYONE NEEDS HIS OR HER OWN IGOR JR. TO BOSS AROUND!

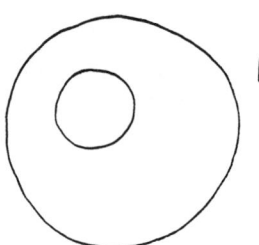

1. Draw a large circle with a smaller circle inside it for Igor Jr.'s one showing eye.

2. Add a large hooked nose and a backward C for his ear.

3. Sketch a chin jutting out from his face, as well as a small, thick eyebrow.

4. Draw a furrowed forehead and a prominent wart on his nose. Add a tiny pupil in his eye.

5. Begin to draw his wavy, stand-up hair. Indicate a neck.

6. Erase the unneeded lines, and fill in his eyebrow. Complete his hair.

 # Monstress Maude

ON YOUR OWN, GIVE MONSTRESS MAUDE A FREAKY BODY ANY LATE-NIGHT CREEP WOULD BE PROUD OF.

1. Begin Maude's head with an egg shape. Add two circles for eyes, with two dots for her pupils. Start her mouth with a horizontal line and a dimple on either side.

2. Finish her mouth, making it open and friendly. Give her short, spiky eyelashes and two ears.

3. Begin to draw her hair, and continue rendering her mouth.

4. Add lips and teeth to her mouth. Draw a neck with two large bolts protruding on either side.

5. Sketch lots of big hair around her face. Finish her neck bolts.

6. Fill in her hair and lips as shown.

Pirate Pete

AYE, MATEY! PIRATE PETE *DARES* YOU TO DRAW A PARROT ON HIS SHOULDER!

1. Draw his head, one large eye, a hooked nose, and an ear.

2. Draw an eye patch on the other side of his nose. Indicate a small downturned mouth, and sketch his neck.

3. Begin to draw his head scarf, and add a pupil in his wide, large eye.

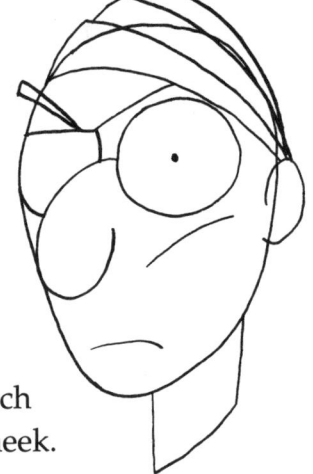

4. Continue drawing his scarf and eye patch. Begin to sketch a deep scar across his left cheek.

5. Finish his scar with small vertical lines. Start to sketch beard stubble across his chin. Continue working on his scarf.

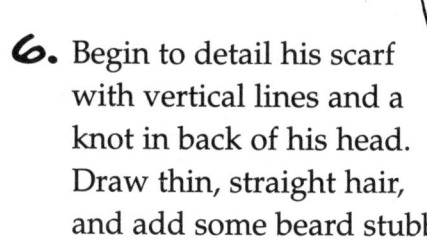

6. Begin to detail his scarf with vertical lines and a knot in back of his head. Draw thin, straight hair, and add some beard stubble.

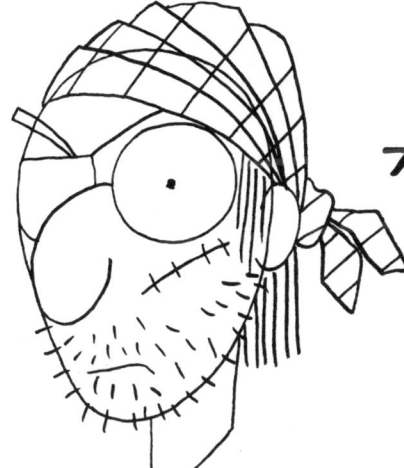

7. Complete his scarf knot.

8. Erase unnecessary lines, and fill in his eye patch.

Val Kyrie

NOBODY CAN SING LIKE VAL KYRIE... THANK GOODNESS!

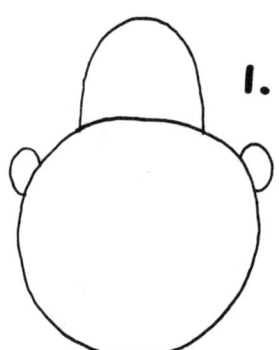

1. Begin Val's head with a circle. Start to draw her Viking headpiece on top, and add two small ears.

2. Draw a horizontal line in her helmet. Add facial details: her closed eyes, eyelashes, and upturned nose. Give her a thin neck.

3. Continue to detail her headpiece. Draw a WIDE, open mouth.

4. Add horns to her headpiece, and draw her upper lip.

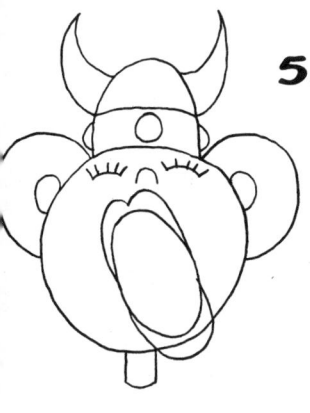

5. Sketch her lower lip, and start to render her hair.

6. Give Val teeth, and continue to draw her hair.

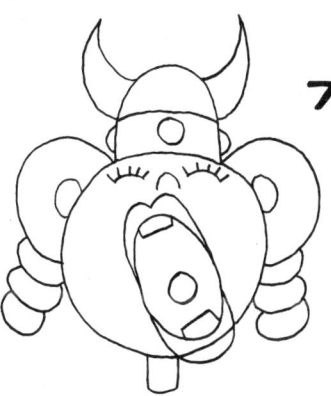

7. Sketch more hair as shown, and draw a small tongue inside her mouth.

8. Detail her tongue, and complete her hair.

9. Erase the unneeded lines, and fill in her mouth.

Grin Kong

NOW, THIS IS ONE GORILLA ANYONE COULD BUDDY AROUND WITH.

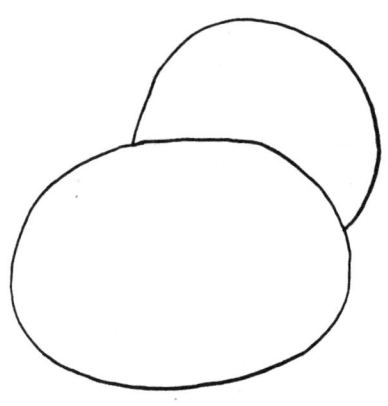

1. Outline the head with the two shapes shown.

2. Draw small round eyes and an ear.

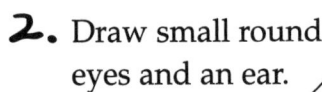

3. Indicate large shoulders on either side of the head. Give Grin Kong a cute pug nose.

4. Begin to draw a snout, with a line coming down from the nose. Further detail the left eye as shown.

5. Continue to work on the snout, and detail the right eye. Draw a small backward C in the ear.

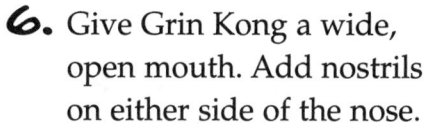

6. Give Grin Kong a wide, open mouth. Add nostrils on either side of the nose.

7. Put pupils in the eyes, and sketch small eyebrows. Draw a line in the mouth to indicate teeth.

8. Sketch three vertical lines in the mouth to complete the teeth. Draw spiky fur on Grin Kong's head.

9. Finish the happy gorilla by erasing any lines you don't need.

Toucan Bill

TOUCAN BILL HAS THE BLUES. AFTER YOU'RE DONE DRAWING HIM, COLOR HIM USING YOUR FAVORITE SHADES OF BLUE.

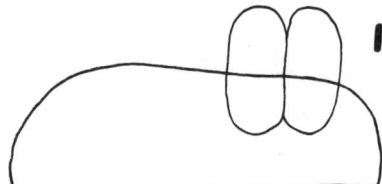

1. Draw an upside-down canoe shape for the large beak. Sketch two ovals next to each other for the eyes.

2. Add two small half-circles for the pupils. Complete the outline of the head with a small half-circle underneath the beak.

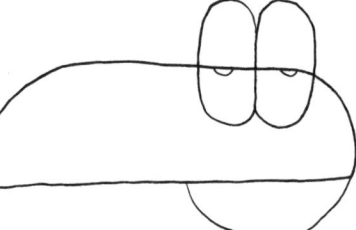

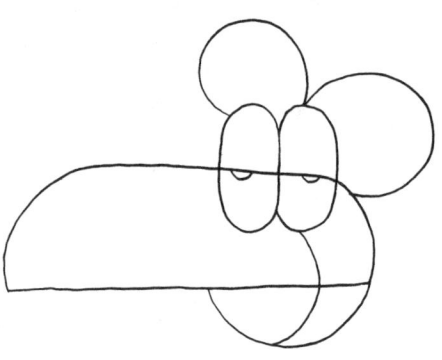

3. Shape the mouth and beak, with a curved shape from the eyes to the chin. Begin to draw fluffy feathers on the head.

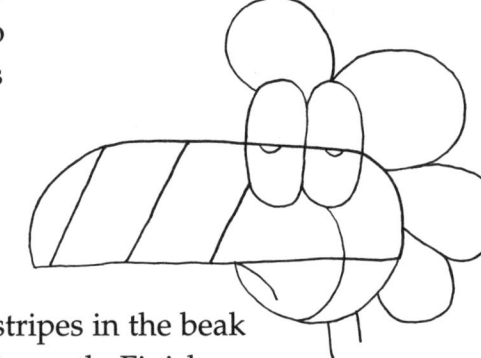

4. Draw a few wide stripes in the beak and a downturned mouth. Finish drawing the feathers, and add a stick neck.

5. Erase unnecessary lines, and fill in the pupils and beak stripes.

 # Bud O'Hare

THIS SILLY RABBIT DOESN'T HAVE HIS OWN TV SERIES, BUT YOU CAN MAKE BUD O'HARE A STAR BY CREATING A CARTOON STRIP WITH HIM.

1. Begin the rabbit with two circles for the chubby cheeks. Add a circle overlapping the cheeks, for the nose. Draw one large tooth coming down from one cheek.

2. Sketch the eyes, unevenly shaped.

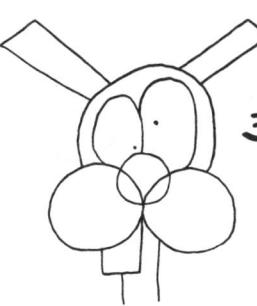

3. Put pupils in the eyes. Begin to draw the ears, and give Bud O'Hare a neck.

4. Finish outlining the ears. Sketch a few small hairs atop the head.

5. Draw the insides of the two ears. Give this bunny whiskers on its cheeks.

6. To finish, erase the unneeded lines in the ears, eyes, and nose. Fill in the nose as shown.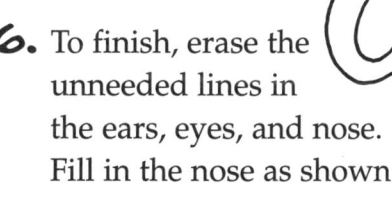

22 Merlo the Mentalist

WATCH OUT—MERLO THE MENTALIST KNOWS ALL!

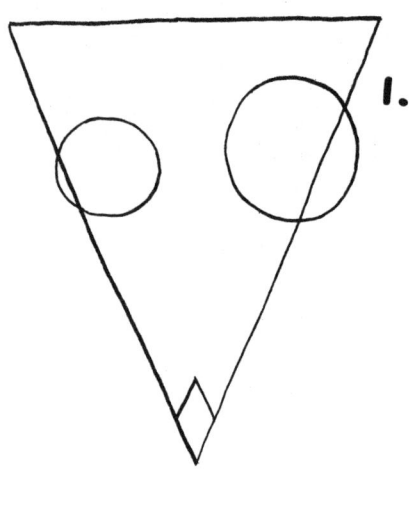

1. Draw an upside-down triangle. Indicate a small diamond in the bottom for his goatee. Sketch two circles, uneven in size, for his eyes.

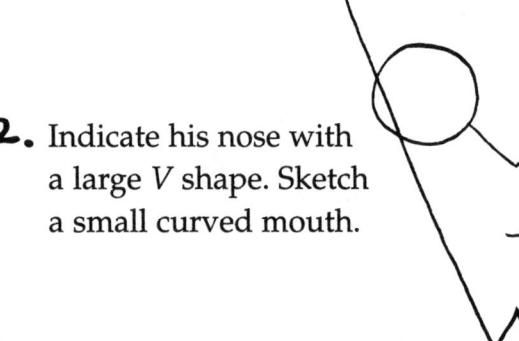

2. Indicate his nose with a large *V* shape. Sketch a small curved mouth.

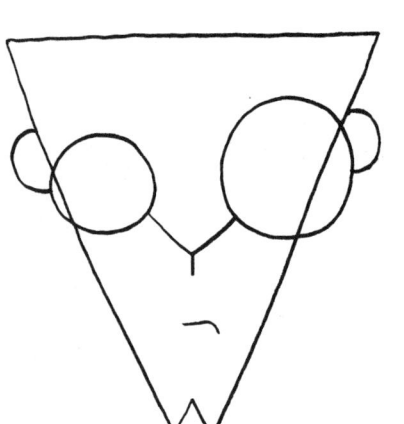

3. Draw a small vertical line coming down from his nose. Add ears.

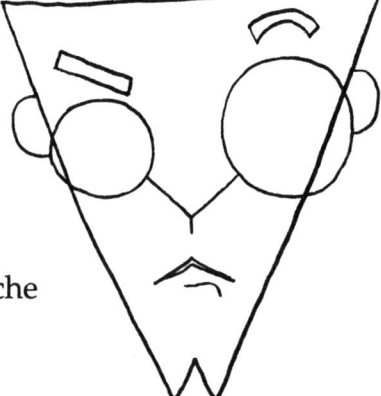

4. Sketch a pencil-thin mustache and two thick eyebrows.

5. Put small Cs in his ears. Sketch a horizontal line in his right eye.

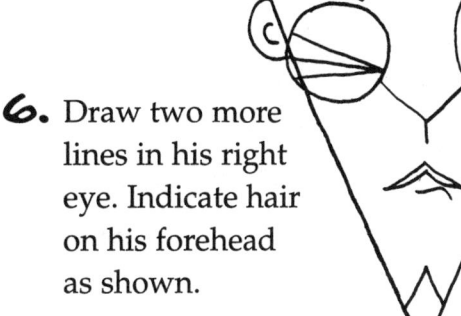

6. Draw two more lines in his right eye. Indicate hair on his forehead as shown.

7. Complete the outline of his hair, and begin to draw a spiral in his left eye.

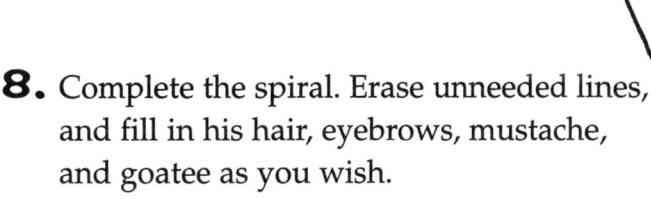

8. Complete the spiral. Erase unneeded lines, and fill in his hair, eyebrows, mustache, and goatee as you wish.

Hard Hat Hank

MAKE THIS GLOOMY CHARACTER SMILE BY GIVING HIM A BODY TO MATCH HIS FUNNY HEAD.

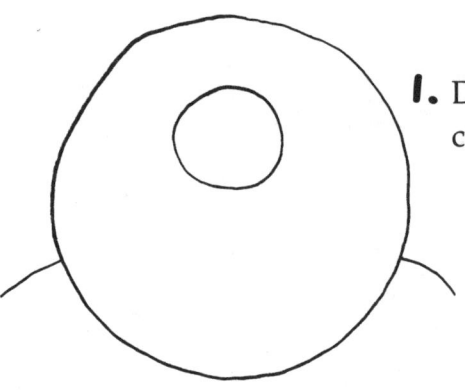

1. Draw a large circle for Hank's head. Add a smaller circle inside it for his nose. Indicate shoulders.

2. Add eyelids and a small downturned mouth. Draw ears.

3. Put pupils in his eyes and nostrils on either side of his nose. Detail the ears, and start to draw his suspenders.

4. Begin to draw his hard hat, and continue working on his suspenders.

5. Sketch the helmet part of his hard hat, and draw a horizontal line connecting his suspenders.

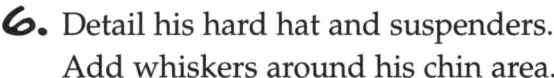

6. Detail his hard hat and suspenders. Add whiskers around his chin area.

7. Give Hank short, spiky hair on top of his head, as well as more whiskers around his chin. Fill in his pupils, and erase unneeded lines in his hard hat.

Sous Chef Sue

THIS SILLY CHEF HAS ONE SPECIALTY—CHOP SUEY!

1. Draw a slightly flattened circle for her head. Sketch eyelids and ears.

2. Add a nose and a wide, open mouth.

3. Continue to render her eyes, mouth, and ears.

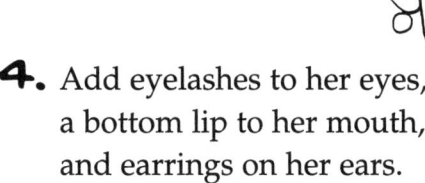

4. Add eyelashes to her eyes, a bottom lip to her mouth, and earrings on her ears.

5. Give Sous Chef Sue eyebrows, as well as pupils in her eyes. Add a horizontal line in her mouth to indicate teeth.

6. Add three vertical lines in her mouth for teeth. Begin to draw her fancy chef's hat.

7. Continue to draw her hat, and sketch curly hair from her hat to her ears.

8. Finish outlining the hat with two more circles on top. Sketch more hair around her face and ears.

9. Erase any unneeded lines. Fill in her eyes, leaving the pupils white. Color in her lips and hair as you wish.

41

Wild-Eyed Wally

DO YOU HAVE ANY FRIENDS LIKE THIS? IF SO, WHEN YOU SEE THEM . . . RUN!

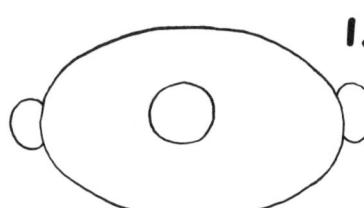

1. Draw a horizontal egg shape, with a circle in its center for Wally's nose. Add two ears.

2. Give him one huge eye and another, much smaller eye.

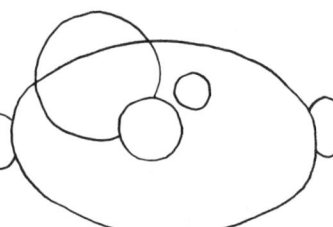

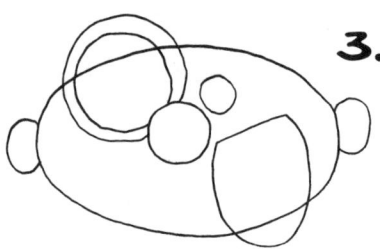

3. Sketch a circle inside his huge eye, and draw a wide, open mouth on one side of his face.

4. Add pupils, and continue to render his mouth with a horizontal line and a curved line for the chin.

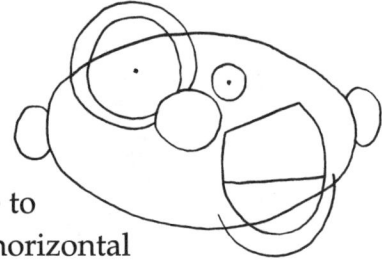

5. Begin to sketch his stand-up hair, as well as his teeth. Add an eyebrow over his small eye.

6. Erase unneeded lines in his mouth, eye, and ears. Complete his kooky hairdo.

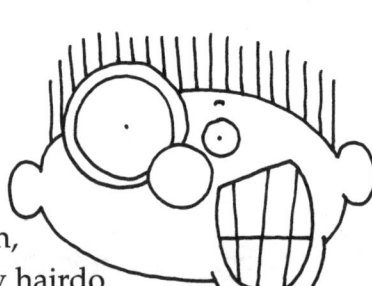

Nikki Nak

WITH A SINGLE BAT OF HER HUGE EYES, NIKKI NAK HAS A KNACK FOR GETTING ANYTHING SHE WANTS.

1. Begin Nikki with a flattened circle, and two huge circles for her eyes.

2. Add an iris and pupil in each eye. Draw ears and a tiny nose.

3. Begin to sketch her heart-shaped lips, and add eyelashes on her top lids.

4. Complete her eyelashes on the bottom lids, then draw her bottom lip. Start drawing her cute flip hairdo.

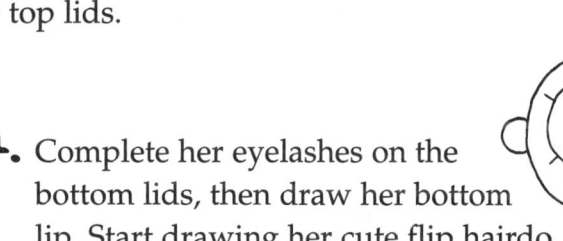

5. Finish the outline of her hair, and give Nikki a little smile.

6. Detail her hair as you wish, and erase any lines you don't need. Fill in her eyes with your favorite color.

Angry Angus

ANGRY ANGUS GETS UPSET OVER EVERYTHING—ESPECIALLY SLOPPY ARTISTS!

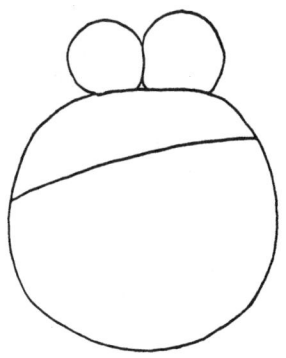

1. Draw a round circle to begin his face. Put two smaller circles on top for his eyes. Add a slightly diagonal line across the large circle.

2. Sketch two diagonal lines in his eyes, both slanted to the center. Draw his nose and nostrils, as well as his ears.

3. Add a few more lines on each eyelid—the more lines, the angrier he is! Draw a smaller diagonal line to show his open mouth. Indicate shoulders.

4. Sketch pupils, teeth, and crazy hair.

5. Begin to draw the smoke that is blowing out of his ears and nostrils.

6. Start to add the smoke puffs to the smoke lines. Begin to add whiskers around his mouth area.

7. Complete the puffs of smoke and whiskers.

8. Fill in the pupils to make Angry Angus look even angrier!

Goof the Clown

A GOOFIER CLOWN YOU'LL NEVER FIND!

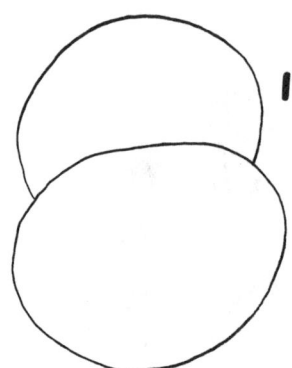

1. Draw a round shape with a partial circle on top of it. This will be Goof the Clown's head.

2. Add a nose and ears.

3. Detail the ears, and sketch eyes.

4. Draw large circles around his eyes, and give Goof a large, friendly mouth.

5. Put pupils in his eyes, add small decorative circles on his cheeks, and sketch a horizontal line in his mouth.

6. Add lines connecting his eyes to the small circles. Put vertical lines in his mouth to detail his teeth.

7. Put an upward curving line in the top of his nose. Outline his mouth.

8. Sketch fun, curly clown hair around his ears and head.

9. Lightly shade around his eyes, nose, and mouth as shown. Fill in his hair as you wish.

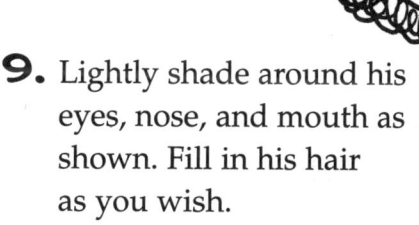

29 King Lou

JUST IMAGINE... KING LOU IS THE *MOST* EXCITING PERSON IN HIS KINGDOM. YIKES!

1. Draw a long oval for King Lou's head. Add eyes, and begin to render his crown.

2. Give him a large nose and an ear.

3. Draw a line down from his nose, ending with a small mouth. Give Lou a neck, and indicate his robe. Add detail to his ear and crown.

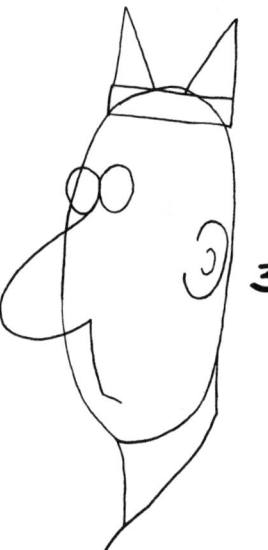

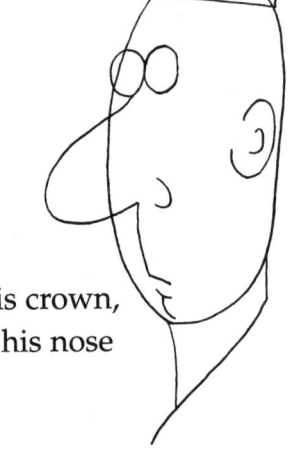

4. Finish outlining his crown, and further detail his nose and mouth area.

5. Add eyebrows, eyelids, and hair.

6. Add a furrowed brow to King Lou's forehead. Sketch pupils in his eyes. Add a hair line under his ear.

7. Further shape his head with more hair in the back. Give his robe a furlike collar.

8. Add small jewels to his crown, and sketch a thin line to show his back.

9. Erase all unnecessary lines, and fill in his hair, pupils, and eyebrows. Detail the robe's collar as you wish.

Pat T. O'Brien

DRAW THIS CUTE CHARACTER IN THE CORNER OF YOUR HOMEWORK TO LIVEN UP ANY BORING ASSIGNMENT.

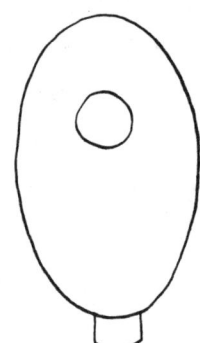

1. Sketch an egg shape for his head. Add a nose and neck.

2. Draw eyelids and ears.

3. Add small pupils and a sideways smile.

4. Indicate a chin with a vertical line under the smile. Begin to draw his hat and bow tie. Add two small lines on his eyes to finish the lids. Give Pat nostrils.

5. Complete his hat, and add bows to his bow tie.

6. Add a line in his hat, and complete his bow tie. Begin to draw hair.

7. Start to draw a cute flower springing from his hat. Finish adding hair. Sketch a stem of grass coming from his mouth.

8. Finish his flower and grass stem.

9. Erase the unnecessary lines. Shade his hair, bow tie, and hat as you wish.

Thrasher Dude

LIKE, THIS IS THE COOLEST CARTOON FACE YOU'LL EVER DRAW, FER SURE!

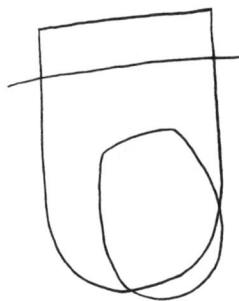

1. Draw a large rectangular shape with the corners rounded on the bottom. Sketch a line across the top of the shape for the top of his sunglasses. Add his big mouth, which is always open.

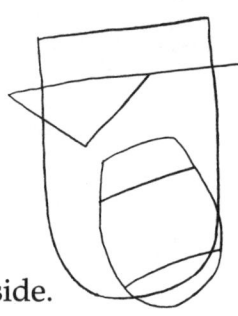

2. Begin to render the sunglasses on one side. Add horizontal lines in his mouth to indicate teeth.

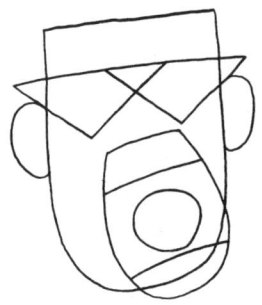

3. Draw the other lens in the sunglasses. Sketch ears, and add a circular tongue in his mouth.

4. Sketch thick eyebrows, and detail his ears. Indicate a chin under his mouth.

5. Detail his tongue and teeth. Draw hair—his is short and spiky here, but you can make it any way you want.

6. Erase the unneeded lines in the sunglasses and mouth. Fill in his eyebrows and mouth, and add a star on his sunglasses.

I. B. Yeller

THIS POOR CREATURE IS AFRAID OF ANYTHING AND EVERYTHING, SO DON'T LEAVE HIM ALONE IN A DARK ROOM.

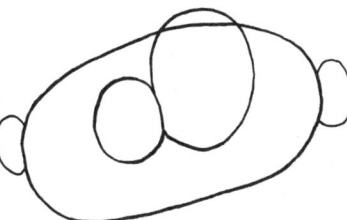

1. Draw a flattened oval for I. B.'s head. Add two eyes, uneven in size. Sketch his ears.

2. Put in two tiny pupils and a large—very large—nose.

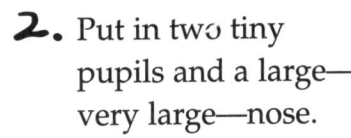

3. Begin to draw his spiky hair. Below his nose, add a mouth.

4. Continue to draw hair, and outline his mouth.

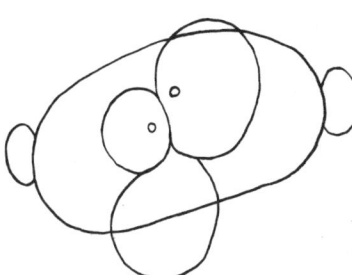

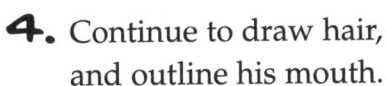

5. Erase any extra lines. Shade in his hair and mouth.

Suzie Q.

THIS LITTLE CHARACTER IS CUTE AS A BUG—IN FACT, MAKE HER EVEN CUTER BY GIVING HER A BUG'S BODY!

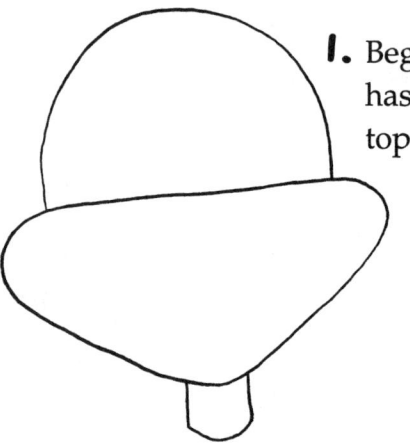

1. Begin with an upside-down triangle that has rounded corners. Add a half-circle on top of it, and give her a neck.

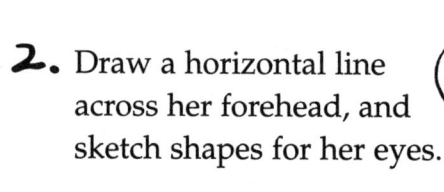

2. Draw a horizontal line across her forehead, and sketch shapes for her eyes.

3. Begin to sketch her hair. Add her eyelids, nose, mouth, and upper lip.

4. Put in her lower lip and large irises.

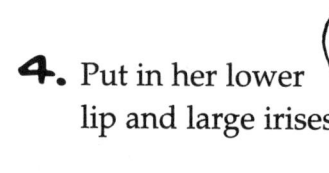

5. Start to outline her hair, and put pupils in the irises of her eyes.

6. Draw small ovals inside her pupils, and finish outlining her hair.

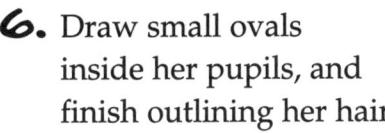

7. Add eyelashes and hair details.

8. Fill in her pupils, leaving the small ovals white. Erase the unneeded lines in her hair and face.

34 The Doctor's Monster 2

THIS GOOFY MONSTER'S HEAD IS ATTACHED TO HIS NECK WITH NUTS AND BOLTS—CAN YOU THINK OF A PERFECT NAME FOR HIM?

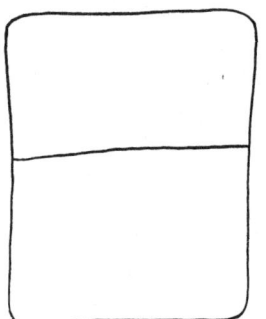

1. Draw a large rectangle with slightly rounded corners. Add a horizontal line running across it.

2. Give your monster a jagged hairline, a boxy mouth with teeth, and two eyes, spaced as shown.

3. Sketch ears and detail them. Put small pupils in his eyes, and draw bulges on either side of his forehead.

4. Draw some additional bulges on the inside of his eyes, and add eyebrows.

5. Connect the inner bulges with a large, flat nose. Draw sagging lines underneath his eyes.

6. Give him a furrowed brow as shown, then draw a thin line running down from his nose.

7. Add another furrowed line on his forehead, and give your monster a neck.

8. Sketch a third and final furrowed line above the other two, and put bolts in the monster's neck.

9. Complete the bolts in his neck, then erase any lines you don't need. Shade his hair, eyebrows, and pupils as you wish.

57

Ye Olde Pilgrim

HE'S A PERFECT ADDITION TO ANY THANKSGIVING CARD YOU SEND.

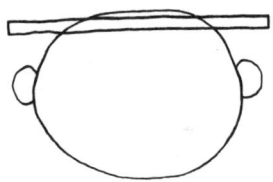

1. Draw a slightly flattened circle. Overlapping the top of it, sketch a thin hat brim. Add two ears.

2. Sketch some hair between the hat brim and ears. Draw two large eyes and a hooked nose. Give your pilgrim a neck and collar.

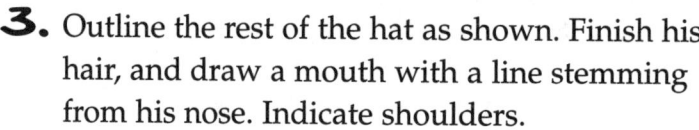

3. Outline the rest of the hat as shown. Finish his hair, and draw a mouth with a line stemming from his nose. Indicate shoulders.

4. Add a thick band on the hat, and draw a thin bow tie. Begin to draw Ye Olde Pilgrim's best friend with two large circles for its eyes.

5. Draw the rest of his friend's head, and indicate a buckle shape on the pilgrim's hat.

6. Complete the buckle on the hat, and give the pilgrim's friend eyebrows and a large hooked beak. Can you tell what his friend is?

7. Put small pupils in the pilgrim's and turkey's eyes. Give the turkey a long, thin neck.

8. Further detail the turkey's beak with two small bumps and a nostril. Separate the beak from the rest of the face.

9. Erase unnecessary lines, and fill in the pilgrim's hat. Detail the turkey's head and neck as shown.

 # Proboscis Pete

PROBOSCIS PETE HAS ONE BIG NOSE! CAN YOU FIGURE OUT WHAT "PROBOSCIS" MEANS?

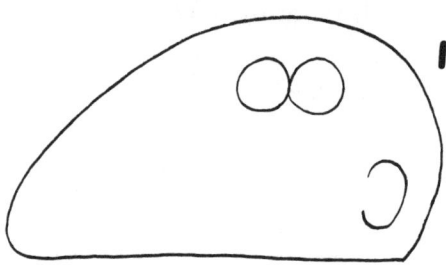

1. Draw an irregular shape with a flat bottom. Add two eyes close together and an ear.

2. Put pupils in his eyes, and begin to draw Pete's spectacles, which are perched on his nose.

3. Start to sketch hair, and finish the spectacles. Add eyebrows, and indicate his rounded chin.

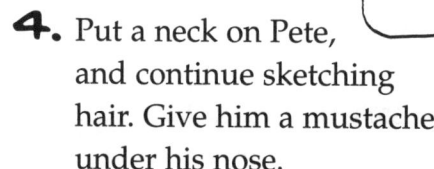

4. Put a neck on Pete, and continue sketching hair. Give him a mustache under his nose.

5. Indicate a *V* neckline, and draw a downturned mouth coming from his chin.

6. Sketch his shoulder and upper arm, and draw a bow tie.

7. Erase the unnecessary lines, then stand back. Pete is ready to blow!

 # Ralphus Cattus

RALPHUS CATTUS LOVES TO RALPH. DON'T FORGET TO INCLUDE SOME COLORFUL VOMIT AROUND THIS FELINE.

 **1.** Draw a long oval shape, flattened on the top. Draw two large humps for his eyes.

2. Add two small triangles for ears, a nose, and a diagonal line for his mouth.

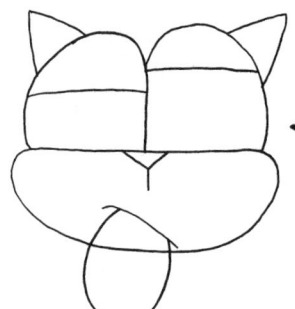 **3.** Give him eyelids at different heights, and continue to render his nose. Sketch a large tongue hanging out of his mouth.

4. Add a tuft of hair sticking up, and put pupils in his eyes. Further detail his ears and tongue.

 **5.** Give Ralphus Cattus zigzag whiskers, and show some droplets falling off his tongue. Fill in his nose, and erase the unnecessary line in his tongue.

Gustavus Goof

YOU COULD CREATE A WHOLE CARTOON STRIP AROUND THIS BIZARRE GUY.

1. Draw a small circle for his head. Add an eye and eyelid on the left and a large shape for his ear on the right.

2. Give him a big upturned nose, and detail his ear.

3. Under his nose, draw a large upper lip. Put a pupil in his eye.

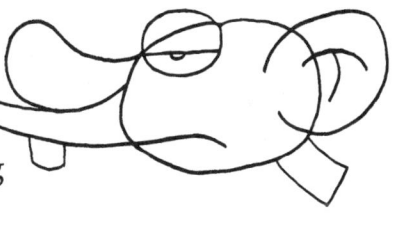

4. Finish detailing his ear, and give Gustavus Goof a neck. Sketch one large tooth sticking out from his upper lip.

5. Give him some scraggly hair, and add another tooth. Indicate his body.

6. Erase all unnecessary lines, and draw his upper arm. Fill in his hair and pupil.

63

Ol' Doc Lang

SKETCH THIS CUTE DOCTOR ON THE NEXT "GET WELL QUICK" CARD YOU SEND.

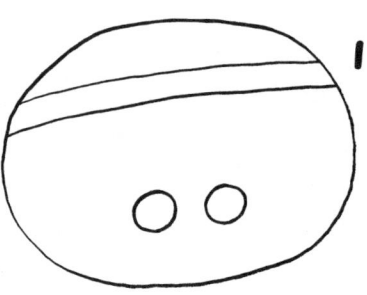

1. Draw a large circle, slightly flattened. Add a band around his forehead, and give him two small lenses for his glasses.

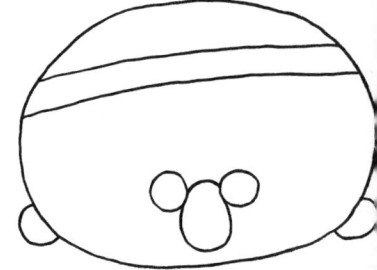

2. Draw his nose, and connect his lenses. Sketch two small ears.

3. Give him eyebrows, pupils, and a large, satisfied smile. Put a light on his forehead band.

4. Sketch a large chin and a neck under his mouth. Detail the light and his ears. Draw hair on the sides of his head.

5. Add some hair on top of his head, and give him a small collar. Erase any lines you don't need. Fill in his eyebrows.

Ho-Hum Henry

THIS GUY MAY SEEM BORING, BUT HE'S REALLY FUN TO DRAW!

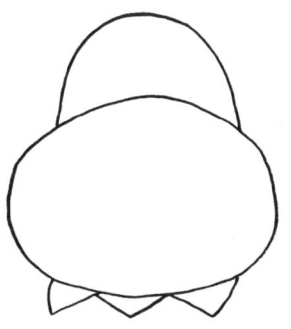

1. Draw an oval on its side. Add a rounded shape on top of it. This will make Henry's head. Add a collar, and start to draw his necktie.

2. Put in Henry's eyes and ears, and complete his necktie.

3. Draw thick eyebrows and a small nose.

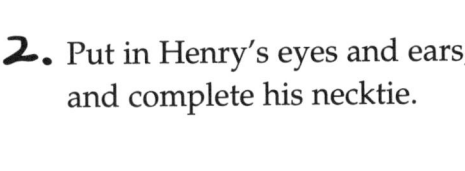

4. Put pupils in his eyes, and detail his ears. Indicate a mouth.

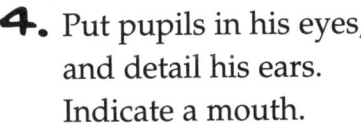

5. Sketch a tuft of hair on top of his head, and add a small line under his mouth to show his chin.

6. Erase the unneeded lines, and fill in his hair, eyebrows, pupils, and necktie.

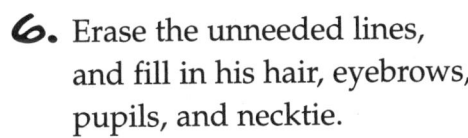

Mrs. Doldrums

MRS. DOLDRUMS AND HO-HUM HENRY ARE GREAT FRIENDS—IMAGINE THEM AT A PARTY!

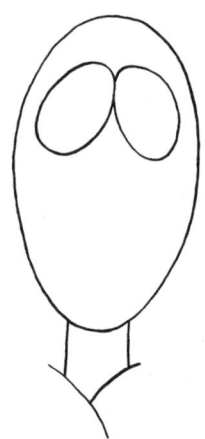

1. Draw a long oval shape, and add two large eyes. Indicate her neck, and start to draw her robe.

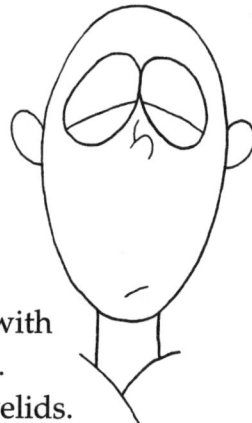

2. Indicate facial features with a nose, mouth, and ears. Draw her half-closed eyelids.

3. Put pupils in her eyes and earrings on her ears. Draw her upper lip.

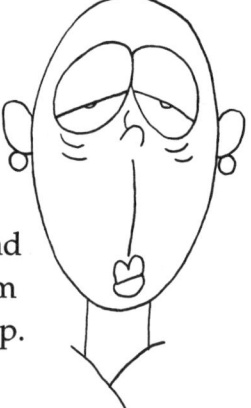

4. Give her some sagging lines under her eyes, and draw a vertical line from her nose to her upper lip. Sketch her bottom lip.

5. Continue to draw her robe, and add eyelashes. Begin to sketch her hair rollers, which she is always wearing.

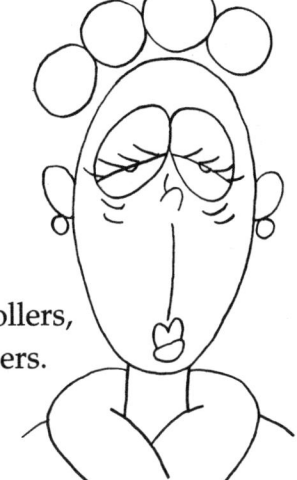

6. Continue to draw her rollers, and indicate her shoulders.

7. Finish outlining her rollers, and put small circles in each one. Start to draw her hair in the rollers.

8. Complete her hair, and fill in her pupils and earrings. Erase the unnecessary lines in her ears.

67

Johnny Angel

PERSONALIZE YOUR OWN ANGEL TO LOOK LIKE YOUR LITTLE SISTER, YOUR BEST FRIEND, OR YOUR FAVORITE PET!

1. Draw a round shape for Johnny's head. Add a hooked nose, and indicate a neck and robe.

2. Sketch eyes and a wide, smiling mouth.

3. Give him eyebrows, ears, and an open mouth.

4. Indicate shoulders, and further detail his mouth and chin.

5. Give Johnny Angel a thick head of hair.

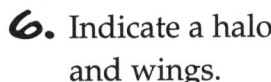

6. Indicate a halo and wings.

7. Outline the halo, and complete his wings. Detail his hair.

8. Erase the unnecessary lines in his ears. Add finishing touches to the halo and wings, and fill in the lower part of his mouth.

Icthyus Imp

THIS CRAZED FISH TAKES ONLY A MINUTE TO DRAW. ADD IT TO A COOL UNDERWATER SCENE.

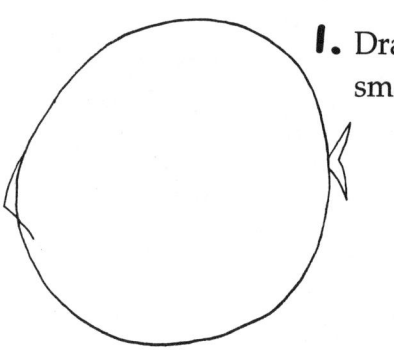

1. Draw a large circle for the fish's body. Add a small mouth in front and a tail fin in back.

2. Sketch fins on top and on the side of the fish. Begin to draw one of its eyes, large and irregular shaped.

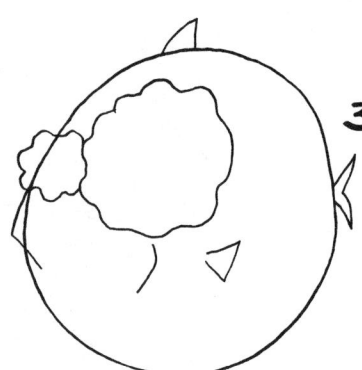

3. Add its other eye, smaller than the first. Indicate a gill below its larger eye.

4. Begin to detail the fins, and add scales. Put a pupil in one eye and a spiraling pupil in the other eye.

5. Add another set of scales, and erase unneeded lines. Don't forget to add tiny bubbles coming up from the fish's mouth.

Skull Twister

SKULL TWISTER *THINKS* HE'S REALLY SCARY—WHAT DO YOU THINK?

1. Draw an irregular round shape with two circles inside it for eye sockets.

2. Add two large ear bumps on the outside edge of the skull. Sketch two rectangles coming down from the skull.

3. Add two more rectangles.

4. Put a crack in the skull, add a nose hole, and sketch two eyes in the eye sockets. Complete the skull with one more rectangle in the center.

5. Place two tiny pupils in the eyes, and add a tongue.

6. Fill in the eye sockets, pupils, and nose hole. Draw a line on the tongue, and erase any extra lines. Add more skull cracks on the top and along the bottom of the head.

'Lectric Man

IMAGINE THE WACKY, SUPER-STRONG BODY YOU CAN ADD TO THIS GUY.

1. Draw a four-sided shape, bigger on the bottom, with rounded corners. Sketch a large *V* in the center, and add a neck.

2. Add the ears and a one-sided mouth.

3. Make his mouth an open grin, and detail his ears. Add a large emblem around his neck. Draw his eyes, one open and the other closed.

4. Indicate his chin, and begin to draw teeth in his mouth.

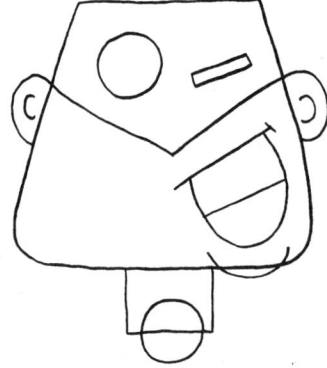

5. Finish drawing his teeth, and start to add full, wavy hair.

6. Continue to sketch his hair, and add his superhero robe.

7. Detail his hair and robe.

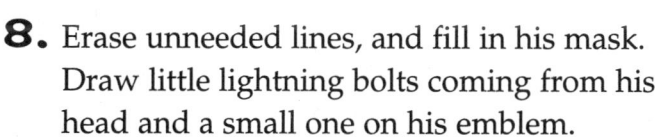

8. Erase unneeded lines, and fill in his mask. Draw little lightning bolts coming from his head and a small one on his emblem.

 # Screamin' Mimi

WHEN SCREAMIN' MIMI SCREAMS, HER CURLY HAIR STRAIGHTENS!

1. Begin with two circles for her eyes. Draw a large round shape for her screaming mouth. Connect her mouth to her eyes as shown, and add a neck.

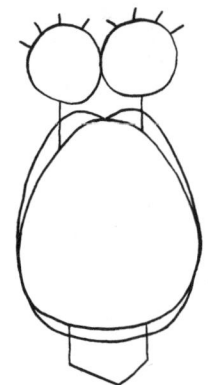

2. Give her eyelashes, and put lips around her mouth.

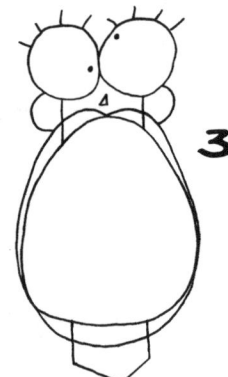

3. Add pupils in her eyes and a small nose. Sketch ears.

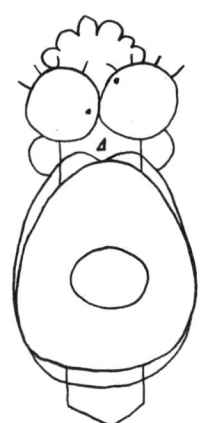

4. Draw some fluffy hair above her eyes. Add a small tongue in her mouth.

5. Detail her ears and tongue, and make her hair stick-straight on the sides.

6. Complete her hair. Erase the unnecessary lines in her lips, and fill in her mouth.

Whistlin' Willy

WHISTLIN' WILLY ONLY WHISTLES BECAUSE HE CAN'T REMEMBER THE WORDS TO ANY TUNES.

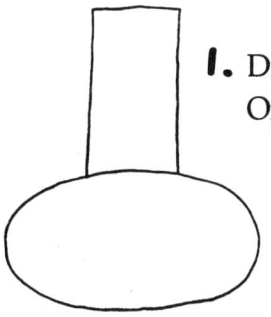

1. Draw a horizontal oval. On top of it, sketch a rectangle.

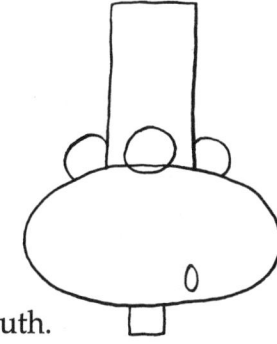

2. Give Willy ears, a nose, a neck, and a small, whistling mouth.

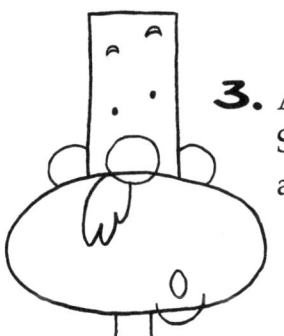

3. Add eyes and eyebrows. Start to draw his mustache, and indicate his chin.

4. Finish his mustache, and draw curved lines around the outsides of his eyes.

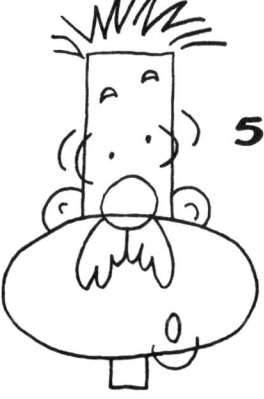

5. Draw another set of curved lines around his eyes, and sketch his wispy hair. Detail his ears.

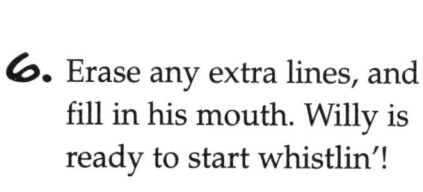

6. Erase any extra lines, and fill in his mouth. Willy is ready to start whistlin'!

Hysterical Hap

CAN YOU DRAW A HYSTERICAL BODY TO MATCH HYSTERICAL HAP'S FACE?

1. Begin with a large circle, and add two unevenly sized eyes on top of it.

2. Sketch ears, and begin to draw a nose.

3. Give Hap pupils in his eyes, and finish drawing his nose.

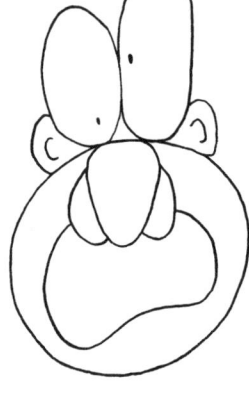

4. Outline Hap's hysterical mouth, and detail his ears.

5. Begin to draw his teeth, and sketch some strands of hair.

6. Continue to draw hair, and put nostrils on his nose.

7. Finish drawing his hair, and add an upper set of teeth.

8. Sketch the whiskers—which are making Hap hysterical—stemming from his nose.

9. Complete this funny face by erasing all unneeded lines and filling in his nostrils and his mouth.

Frannie Fan

FRANNIE FAN IS HER OWN BIGGEST FAN!

1. Draw an upside-down triangle with the corners rounded. Draw a half-circle on top of it. This is the shape of her head. Add two eyes, a mouth, and a neck.

2. Turn her mouth into an open grin, and add a tiny triangle for a nose. Begin to sketch her eyebrows.

3. Put pupils in her eyes, and add a top lip to her mouth. Inside her mouth, indicate teeth with a horizontal line.

4. Continue to render her eyebrows. Sketch her bottom lip.

5. Start to draw her baseball cap, which is on backward. Add a small crease on her forehead.

6. Add a small button on top of her hat, and begin to draw her hair.

7. Continue to sketch her cap, and add more hair.

8. Draw three small holes around her cap, as well as the cap's brim. Sketch more hair.

9. Fill in the cap's brim, Fran's lips, her eyebrows, and the area around her pupils. Erase any lines you don't need. Detail her hair as shown.

Hairy Dan

HAIRY DAN IS THE SILLIEST MAN—HIS MUSTACHE IS SO LONG, HE CAN'T GO NEAR A FAN!

1. To begin, draw a small circle for his nose.

2. Sketch two curlicue lines coming out of either side of his nose for his mustache.

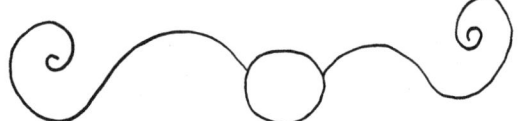

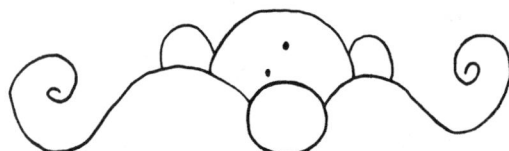

3. Draw a half-circle on top of the nose for Dan's small head. Add two cockeyed eyes and two ears.

4. Finish outlining his mustache, and detail his ears.

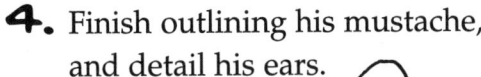

5. Add thin hair on top of his head, and detail his mustache. Give him a thin neck. Add slightly curving lines around his eyes.